Gold

and the Elements of Groups 8 to 12

THE PERIODIC TABLE

Nigel Saunders

Heinemann Library
Chicago, Illinois

Design: David Poole and Tinstar Design Limited
    (www.tinstar.co.uk)
Illustrations: Geoff Ward and Paul Fellows
Picture Research: Rosie Garai
Originated by Bleinheim Colour Ltd.
Printed China by South China Printing Company

07 06 05 04 03
10 9 8 7 6 5 4 3 2 1

**Library of Congress Cataloging-in-Publication
Data**

Saunders, N. (Nigel)
  Gold and the elements of groups 8 to 12 / Nigel
Saunders.
      p. cm. -- (The periodic table)
Summary: Provides an overview of the periodic
table, particularly gold and certain other metals,
describing where these elements are found, how
their atomic numbers are assigned, and uses for
each element.
Includes bibliographical references and index.
  ISBN 1-4034-0871-8 (lib. bdg.) -- ISBN 1-4034-
3517-0 (pbk.)
  1. Metals--Juvenile literature. [1. Metals. 2.
Chemical elements.] I. Title. II. Series.
  QD171.S28 2003
  669
                        2003001072

Acknowledgments
The author and publishers are grateful to the
following for permission to reproduce copyright
material:

pp. **4, 16** James L Amos/Corbis; p. **11** Astrid &
Hans-Frieder Michler/Science Photo Library; p. **13**
BSIP, SERCOM/Science Photo Library; p. **15** D. Van
Ravenswaay/Science Photo Library; p. **18** David
Parker/Science Photo Library; p. **20** Sinclair
Stammers/Science Photo Library; p. **21** Kevin R.
Morris/Corbis; p. **23** Ancient Art & Architecture;
pp. **24, 35, 48** Photodisc; p. **25** Action Plus; p. **26**
Russ Lappa/Science Photo Library; p. **27** Royal
Ontario Museum/Corbis; pp. **29, 32, 40** (bottom)
Trevor Clifford; p. **30** Klaus Guldbrandsen/Science
Photo Library; pp. **31, 39** Chris Collins/Corbis; p.
33 Science Museum/Science Photo Library; p. **34**
Kaj R. Svensson/Science Photo Library; p. **37** Diy
Photo Library; p. **38** Pascal Goetgheluck/Science
Photo Library; p. **41** (top) Stapleton
Collection/Corbis; pp. **42, 43** Roger Garwood &
Trish Ainslie/Corbis; p. **44** NASA/Science Photo
Library; pp. **46, 50, 51** Russ Lappa/Science Photo
Library; p. **47**; p. **49** rud-gr.com/ Zefa; p. **52** Rolls
Royce; pp. **53, 55** Tudor Photography; p. **54** Alfred
Pasieka/Science Photo Library; p. **57** Michael S.
Yamashita/Corbis.

Cover photograph of the gold bars and nuggets
reproduced with permission of Getty Images.

The publishers would like to thank Theodore Dolter
for his review of this book.

The author would like to thank Angela, Kathryn,
David and Jean for all their help and support.

Every effort has been made to contact copyright
holders of any material reproduced in this book.
Any omissions will be rectified in subsequent
printings if notice is given to the publishers.

Disclaimer
All the Internet addresses (URLs) given in this
book were valid at the time of going to press.
However, due to the dynamic nature of the
Internet, some addresses may have changed, or
sites may have ceased to exist since publication.
While the author and publishers regret any
inconvenience this may cause readers, no
responsibility for any such changes can be
accepted by either the author or the publishers.

Words appearing in bold, **like this,** are
explained in the Glossary.

Contents

Elements and Atomic Structure

Have you ever wondered how many different substances there are in the world? If you look around, you will see metals, plastics, water, and lots of other solids and liquids. You cannot see the gases in the air, but you know they are there, and there are many other gases, too. So just how many different substances are there? Incredibly, more than 19 million different substances have been discovered, named, and cataloged. Around 4,000 substances are added to the list each day. All these substances are made from just a few simple substances called **elements.**

Elements

There are about 90 naturally occurring elements as well as a few artificial ones. Elements are substances that cannot be broken down into simpler substances using chemical **reactions.** About three-quarters of the elements are metals, such as copper and gold, and most of the rest are nonmetals, such as sulfur and oxygen. Some elements, like germanium, are called metalloids because they have some of the properties of metals and some of the properties of nonmetals.

Compounds

Elements can join together in chemical reactions to make **compounds.** For example, copper and oxygen react together to make copper oxide, and sulfur and oxygen react together to make sulfur dioxide. Nearly all of the millions of different substances in the world are compounds, made up of two or more elements chemically joined together.

These sailboards are made from some of the millions of known chemicals, including plastics and metals. Seawater and clouds are made from chemicals—and so are the surfers!

Atoms

Every substance is made up of tiny particles called **atoms.** An element is made up of just one type of atom, and a compound is made up of two or more types of atoms joined together. Atoms are far too small to see, even with an **electron** microscope. If you could line up copper atoms side by side along a 6-inch (15-centimeter) ruler, you would need over 535 million of them!

Atoms themselves are made up of even tinier **subatomic particles** called **protons, neutrons,** and electrons. At the center of each atom, there is a **nucleus** made up of protons and neutrons. The electrons are arranged in different energy levels around the nucleus. Most of an atom is actually empty space—if an atom were blown up to the same size as an Olympic running track, its nucleus would be about the size of a pea! The electrons, and how they are arranged, are responsible for the ways in which each element can react.

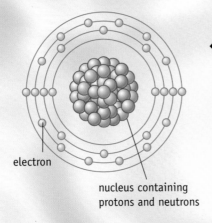

This model shows an atom of iron. Each iron atom nucleus contains 26 protons and 30 neutrons, and its 26 electrons are arranged in four shells around the nucleus.

electron

nucleus containing
protons and neutrons

Elements and groups

Different elements react with other substances in different ways. Scientists found it difficult to make sense of these chemical reactions. In 1869, a Russian chemist named Dimitri Mendeleev put each element into one of eight **groups** in a table. Each group contained elements with similar chemical properties. This made it easier for chemists to figure out what to expect when they reacted elements with each other. You can find the modern **periodic table** on the next page.

The Periodic Table and the Transition Metals

Chemists built on Mendeleev's work and eventually produced the modern **periodic table,** seen here. Each row in the table is called a **period,** and the **elements** in a period are arranged in order of increasing **atomic number** (the atomic number is the number of **protons** in the **nucleus**). Each column in the table is called a **group.** The elements in each group have similar chemical properties. For example, the elements in group 1 are very reactive, soft metals, and the elements in group 18 are very unreactive gases. However, some groups, like group 13, contain both metals and nonmetals. It is called the periodic table because these different chemical properties occur regularly, or periodically.

The elements in a group are usually very similar to each other. This makes it easier to learn about the different elements because you do not have to remember details about each one—you just have to remember the things that apply to a group and the trends in it. However, the transition metals are a bit different.

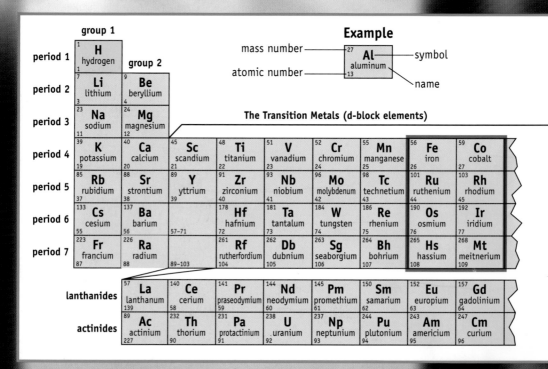

The transition metals

The transition metals are the big block of elements in the middle of the periodic table, from group 3 to group 12. They have many properties in common, such as high melting and boiling points, but they are not identical to each other. Tungsten, for example, has the highest melting point of any metal, while mercury is the only metal that is a liquid at room temperature. The transition metals tend to have high **densities,** and they often produce colored **compounds.** Unlike the other elements in the periodic table, the transition metals in each group may be less like each other, and more like the elements to either side of them. However, they do have some things in common, such as the formulas of the compounds they form with other elements.

In this book, you will find out about iron, nickel, gold, and the other transition metals in the second five groups, as well as the compounds they make and many of their uses.

▼ *This is the periodic table of the elements. The transition metals consist of ten groups of elements that lie between group 2 and group 13.*

Key

- metals
- metalloids
- nonmetals

			group 13	group 14	group 15	group 16	group 17	group 18	
								4 **He** helium 2	period 1
			11 **B** boron 5	12 **C** carbon 6	14 **N** nitrogen 7	16 **O** oxygen 8	19 **F** fluorine 9	20 **Ne** neon 10	period 2
			27 **Al** aluminum 13	28 **Si** silicon 14	31 **P** phosphorus 15	32 **S** sulfur 16	35 **Cl** chlorine 17	40 **Ar** argon 18	period 3
59 **Ni** nickel 28	64 **Cu** copper 29	65 **Zn** zinc 30	70 **Ga** gallium 31	73 **Ge** germanium 32	75 **As** arsenic 33	79 **Se** selenium 34	80 **Br** bromine 35	84 **Kr** krypton 36	period 4
106 **Pd** palladium 46	108 **Ag** silver 47	112 **Cd** cadmium 48	115 **In** indium 49	119 **Sn** tin 50	122 **Sb** antimony 51	128 **Te** tellurium 52	127 **I** iodine 53	131 **Xe** xenon 54	period 5
195 **Pt** platinum 78	197 **Au** gold 79	201 **Hg** mercury 80	204 **Tl** thallium 81	207 **Pb** lead 82	209 **Bi** bismuth 83	209 **Po** polonium 84	210 **At** astatine 85	222 **Rn** radon 86	period 6
269 **Uun** ununnilium 110	272 **Uuu** unununium 111	269 **Uub** ununbium 112		289 **Uuq** ununquadium 114		292 **Uuh** ununhexium 116			period 7

159 **Tb** terbium 65	163 **Dy** dysprosium 66	165 **Ho** holmium 67	167 **Er** erbium 68	169 **Tm** thulium 69	173 **Yb** ytterbium 70	175 **Lu** lutetium 71	
247 **Bk** berkelium 97	251 **Cf** californium 98	252 **Es** einsteinium 99	257 **Fm** fermium 100	258 **Md** mendelevium 101	259 **No** nobelium 102	262 **Lr** lawrencium 103	f block

General Features of the Transition Metals

The transition metals are good conductors of electricity and heat. They tend to be hard, strong, and tough. Most of them are **malleable,** meaning that they are easily bent or hammered into shape. The transition metals are very similar to each other. This is because, apart from zinc, cadmium, and mercury in **group** 12, part of one of their outer **electron** shells is not completely filled with electrons. This is called the d subshell, and the transition metals belong to a block of **elements** in the **periodic table** called the d-block.

Most of the other familiar metals are in groups 1 and 2, so it is helpful to see how the transition metals compare with them. Group 1 includes lithium, sodium, and potassium, and group 2 includes magnesium and calcium.

High melting and boiling points
Nearly all the transition metals have higher melting and boiling points than the metals in groups 1 and 2. Only zinc, cadmium, and mercury melt or boil at lower temperatures.

The boiling points of nearly all the transition metals are much higher than the boiling points of the metals in group 2. The melting points of the metals in group 1 are even lower. ▶

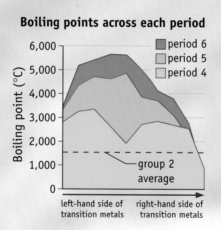

Boiling points across each period

y-axis: Boiling point (°C) — 0, 1,000, 2,000, 3,000, 4,000, 5,000, 6,000

Legend: period 6, period 5, period 4

group 2 average

left-hand side of transition metals   right-hand side of transition metals

High densities
The elements in groups 1 and 2 have low **densities.** Lithium, sodium, and potassium can even float on water, but transition metals generally have high densities. Osmium and iridium have the highest densities of any element, and just 3 liters (3.17 quarts) of them have the mass of an average adult man!

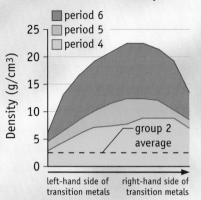

Densities across each period

- period 6
- period 5
- period 4

Density (g/cm³)

25
20
15
10
5
0

group 2 average

left-hand side of transition metals

right-hand side of transition metals

The densities of all the transition metals are much higher than the densities of the metals in group 2. The densities of the metals in group 1 are even lower.

Catalysts and colors

Metals lose electrons from their outer shells when they react with nonmetals, such as oxygen. When they do this, they form electrically charged particles called **ions.** Metal ions are positively charged. Group 1 metals always form ions with a single positive charge, like the Na^+ ions formed by sodium. Group 2 metals always form ions with two positive charges, such as magnesium ions, Mg^{2+}. However, transition metals can form more than one type of ion. As a result, transition metals and their **compounds** frequently make good **catalysts,** meaning that they can speed up **reactions** without being used up.

Transition metals can also form different compounds with the same nonmetal. For example, iron and oxygen react together to make iron oxide. However, there are several forms of it, so chemists use roman numbers to tell them apart. FeO is iron (II) oxide ("iron two oxide") and it contains Fe^{2+} ions. However, Fe_2O_3 is iron (III) oxide ("iron three oxide") and it contain Fe^{3+} ions. Transition metal compounds are usually colored because of the way light is absorbed by the electrons in them. Iron (II) oxide is black, but iron (III) oxide is red-brown.

The Platinum Group Metals

There are six transition metals that are particularly similar to each other. These are ruthenium, osmium, rhodium, iridium, palladium, and platinum. They form a block in the middle of the transition metals and are called the platinum **group** metals after the most abundant member of the group. As you will discover, they are very similar in many ways.

The platinum group metals are extremely rare in Earth's crust. On average, there is only a gram (0.035 ounce) of ruthenium in each ton of rock, and barely a gram of rhodium in over 1,000 tons of rock! There are few **minerals** that contain platinum group metals in worthwhile amounts, and they are found mostly in South Africa and Russia. Wastes produced from nickel **refining** are also a source of these metals.

Not only are the platinum group metals very similar to each other, they are often mixed together to form natural **alloys,** such as osmiridium (osmium and iridium) and platiniridium (platinum and iridium). This makes it difficult to separate them from one another. However, they are very useful in the manufacture of a variety of highly specialized items.

Catalytic converters

When a hydrocarbon like gasoline burns completely in oxygen, the only **products** are carbon dioxide and water vapor. However, in a car engine, the amount of air is limited and some of the fuel does not burn completely. As a result, it also produces carbon monoxide and unburned hydrocarbons, called **volatile** organic **compounds,** or VOCs. In addition, nitrogen and oxygen in the air **react** together in the hot engine to produce nitrogen oxides, called NOx. These gases pollute the atmosphere when they escape through the exhaust pipe. Carbon monoxide is a poisonous gas, VOCs can react with other gases in the air to cause smog, and NOx can dissolve in clouds to cause acid rain. Car exhaust systems are fitted with catalytic converters to change these harmful gases into less harmful ones.

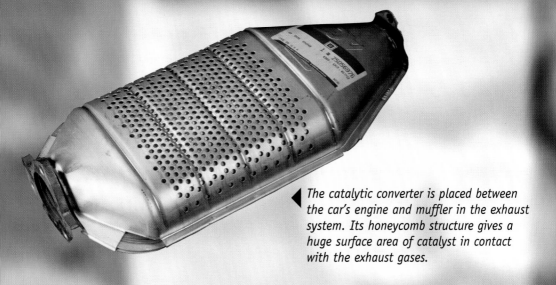

The catalytic converter is placed between the car's engine and muffler in the exhaust system. Its honeycomb structure gives a huge surface area of catalyst in contact with the exhaust gases.

A catalytic converter is a stainless steel can placed between the engine and the muffler. The **catalyst** inside is made from platinum, rhodium, and palladium alloys. Catalytic converters use 41 percent of the world's production of platinum, 98 percent of its rhodium, and 70 percent of its palladium. These are expensive metals because they are so rare. To reduce the cost and to provide a big surface area for the gases to react on, the catalysts are coated onto a **ceramic** honeycomb. The polluting gases are converted into less harmful nitrogen, carbon dioxide, and water vapor as they pass through the converter. A modern three-way catalytic converter reduces the three types of polluting gases by up to 90 percent.

Equations for some of the catalytic converter reactions are:

nitrogen + carbon → nitrogen + carbon
oxides   monoxide   dioxide

$$N_2O(g) + CO(g) \rightarrow N_2(g) + CO_2(g)$$

carbon monoxide + oxygen → carbon dioxide

$$2CO(g) + O_2(g) \rightarrow 2CO_2(g)$$

unburned hydrocarbons + oxygen → carbon + water
(VOCs)   dioxide

$$C_7H_{16}(l) + 11O_2(g) \rightarrow 7CO_2(g) + 8H_2O(l)$$

Group 8: Ruthenium and Osmium

101	
Ru	
ruthenium	
44	

ruthenium
symbol: Ru • atomic number: 44 • period 5

Ruthenium is a hard, white metal that will **react** with oxygen only when it is heated strongly. Ruthenium does not react with water or acids, or even with a powerful mixture of concentrated hydrochloric acid and nitric acid called **aqua regia.**

Ruthenium was first discovered in 1828 by Gottfried Osann, a chemist working at the University of Tartu in Estonia. He named it after the Latin name for Russia. Unfortunately, Osann took back his claim after Jöns Berzelius, the Swedish chemist who had isolated titanium three years earlier, could not confirm his discovery. In 1844, a Russian chemist named Karl Klaus managed to isolate several grams of ruthenium, so he is usually given the credit for discovering it.

Less than a ton of ruthenium is produced each year. It is used in electronic components called resistors, and it is found in many electrical devices, including computers and mobile phones. Hard disk drives in computers store information on disks that are coated with a magnetic material. The amount of information that can be stored can be increased enormously by adding a layer of ruthenium just three **atoms** thick!

Ruthenium and its **compounds** are important **catalysts** used by the oil industry to remove smelly hydrogen sulfide from oil.

190	
Os	
osmium	
76	

osmium
symbol: Os • atomic number: 76 • period 6

Osmium is a hard, **brittle** metal with a tinge of blue. It is probably the **densest** element, although iridium has a very similar density. Osmium does not react with water or acids, or even with aqua regia. It reacts with oxygen in the air at room temperature to produce osmium (VIII) oxide. This is a solid, but it easily turns into a smelly vapor.

In 1803, an English chemist named Smithson Tennant discovered and isolated osmium from a sample of impure platinum. He named the new **element** after the Greek word for smell, because of the awful smell made when osmium reacts with the air.

Only about 330 pounds (150 kilograms) of osmium are produced each year. Its main use is in **alloys** with other platinum **group** metals and gold, because it makes them much harder. These alloys are used to make tough pen tips and parts for scientific instruments.

Biologists use osmium (VIII) oxide to prepare specimens for examination using a microscope. To get enough light through a specimen, it must be cut into a very thin slice and stained for anything to show up. Before a specimen can be stained, it must be "fixed" to stop the cells from changing shape. Osmium (VIII) oxide reacts with the fats in cell membranes and fixes them. When it does this, it turns into black osmium (IV) oxide and stains the specimen as well, so it can be examined using a light microscope. Osmium also shows up in **electron** microscope pictures because it is very dense.

▼ *This is a blood platelet as seen through a transmission electron microscope. You cannot see the membrane itself, just the outline of it where the osmium (VIII) oxide has reacted and stuck to it.*

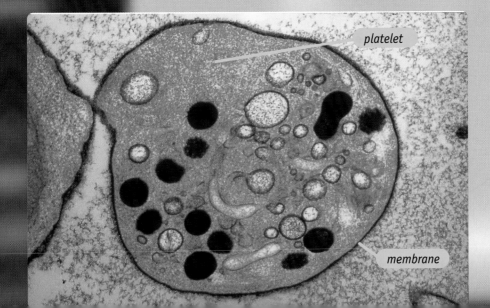

platelet

membrane

Group 9: Rhodium and Iridium

103 Rh rhodium 45	**rhodium** *symbol: Rh • atomic number: 45 • period 5*

Rhodium is a hard, silvery metal. It does not **react** with water, and it reacts with oxygen only when heated strongly. Rhodium does not react with acids, including **aqua regia.**

An English chemist named William Wollaston discovered and isolated rhodium in 1803 from a sample of impure platinum. One of the rhodium **compounds** Wollaston made was red, so he named the new metal after the Greek word for rose-colored.

Although only about 20 tons of rhodium are produced each year, it is an important metal. Nearly all of it is used in catalytic converters, but a rhodium–platinum **alloy** is used as the **catalyst** for the industrial production of nitric acid from ammonia. Small amounts of rhodium are often added to platinum and palladium to make alloys that are tougher than the metals on their own. Because these alloys have high melting points and are very unreactive, they are widely used to make laboratory equipment such as crucibles.

192 Ir iridium 77	**iridium** *symbol: Ir • atomic number: 77 • period 6*

Iridium is a silvery-white metal that reacts with air only when it is heated, forming black iridium oxide. It does not react with water or acids, or even with aqua regia.

Smithson Tennant, the English chemist who discovered osmium in 1803, also discovered and isolated iridium the following year, from a sample of impure platinum. Because iridium makes colorful compounds, it is named after Iris, the ancient Greek goddess of rainbows.

Iridium is the most **corrosion**-resistant metal of all, but it is difficult to work into shape because it is very hard and **brittle.** As a result, it is usually mixed with platinum to make tough alloys that do not corrode. These alloys are used to make surgical instruments, crucibles for chemists to analyze chemicals, electrical contacts, and spark plugs for car engines.

Dinosaurs, meteorites, and iridium

Scientists believe iridium may have played a part in the destruction of the dinosaurs. The concentration of iridium in meteorites is over a thousand times more than its concentration in Earth's crust, and meteorites release a lot of iridium when they crash through the atmosphere into the ground. This iridium eventually settles on the ground, and gives scientists a big clue about when a meteorite might have hit Earth in the past, and where.

The dinosaurs died out at the end of the Cretaceous period, and there is a lot of iridium in the layer between the rocks from the Cretaceous period and the Tertiary period just after that. Some scientists think that this iridium at the boundary shows that a very large meteorite hit Earth about 65 million years ago. The impact would have thrown up lots of dust into the atmosphere, affecting the climate and helping to drive the dinosaurs to extinction.

This shows how the Chicxulub basin in the Yucatán peninsula of Mexico might have looked soon after impact. The 186-mi (300-km) crater has since been filled in.

106	
Pd	**palladium**
palladium	*symbol: Pd • atomic number: 46 • period 5*
46	

Palladium is a soft, steel-gray metal. It is the most reactive of the platinum **group** metals, and it **reacts** slowly with concentrated acids. However, it does not react with water, and it reacts with oxygen only when it is heated. Palladium can **adsorb** huge amounts of hydrogen gas on its surface. This gas can be released later just by heating the metal.

English chemist William Wollaston discovered and isolated palladium in 1803 from a sample of impure platinum. He named it in honor of Pallas (the second largest asteroid), that had only just been found the year before.

These platinum coins were minted in Russia between 1825 and 1855. The platinum was mined in the Ural Mountains, lying between Europe and Asia.

Around 200 tons of palladium are produced each year. It is used in electronic devices, jewelry, and dental bridges and caps. However, most of it is used as a **catalyst.** Palladium's biggest single use as a catalyst is in catalytic converters for car exhaust. It works particularly well in hydrogenation reactions, in which hydrogen is added to other chemicals. Palladium is the catalyst used to produce hydrogen peroxide, a substance that is widely used in the chemical and papermaking industries.

| 195 Pt platinum 78 | **platinum** symbol: Pt • atomic number: 78 • period 6 |

Platinum is a very unreactive, silvery metal. It reacts with **aqua regia,** but it does not react with other acids, air, or water.

The people living in Central America used platinum to make jewelry long before Christopher Columbus discovered America in the 15th century. A Spanish explorer named Antonio de Ulloa described platinum in his journal in 1735, so he is given the credit for its discovery even though the local people had been using it for centuries. In 1805, William Wollaston developed a method to produce platinum in a form that was easy to work with, but he kept his method a secret until 1828, eventually becoming a wealthy man as a result.

Jewelry and catalytic converters are the two biggest uses of platinum, accounting for about 150 tons of the metal each year. A platinum **bullion** coin or bar costs about twice as much as the same mass of gold. Like gold, platinum does not tarnish, but, unlike gold, it is strong and even very fine pieces keep their shape well. This makes platinum ideal for jewelry—if you can afford it! Platinum in jewelry is usually 95 percent platinum **alloyed** with copper and other platinum group metals. It can be polished to a highly reflective and attractive finish. About 1 percent of platinum is hoarded away as bullion coins and bars, but about 40 percent is made into jewelry.

Although less important in terms of the amount of metal used, platinum is also used in electronic devices and to make different types of laboratory equipment. Cisplatin, a platinum **compound,** has been used as an important anticancer drug.

The Artificial Transition Metals

Uranium **atoms** are the heaviest natural atoms, with 92 **protons** in their **nuclei.** Atoms with more protons, called transuranic **elements,** have to be made artificially by converting one element into another. The ancient alchemists had tried to turn lead into gold without any success. This was because it is not possible to convert one element into another by chemical **reactions**—you can turn one element into another only by a nuclear reaction.

When a **radioactive** atom **decays,** its nucleus splits apart to make a new nucleus and **radiation.** The new element made has a smaller number of particles in its nucleus than the original element. To get a new artificial element with a bigger nucleus, you need to smash **ions** into a metal target at high speed and hope that some of them will stick together. Nine artificial transition metals have been made this way, but the amounts are so tiny, often just a few atoms, that very little is known about their chemistry. However, chemists predict that they will have properties similar to those of the other transition metals.

129 **Hs** hassium 108	**hassium** symbol: Hs • atomic number: 108 • period 7

Hassium was made in 1984 when scientists fired iron ions at a lead target. Over ten days, they managed to produce just three atoms of hassium! Their research was carried out in Darmstadt, in the German state of Hesse, and hassium comes from the Latin name for Hesse. Until 1997, hassium was called unniloctium (pronounced yoon-nil-oct-ee-um), meaning "one-zero-eight."

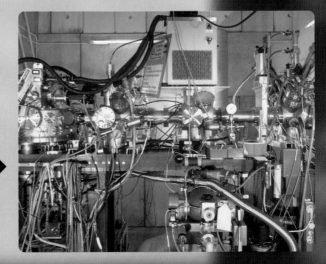

Many of the artificial transition metals were made here at the Institute for Heavy Ion Research in Darmstadt, Germany.

| 268 **Mt** meitnerium 109 | **meitnerium** *symbol: Mt • atomic number: 109 • period 7* |

The German team that made hassium was also the first to make meitnerium. They smashed iron ions into a bismuth target over ten days, and succeeded in making a single atom of meitnerium in 1982. The new element was named after one of the discoverers of atomic fission, an Austrian-Swedish physicist named Lise Meitner. Until 1997, it was temporarily called unnilennium (pronounced yoon-nil-en-ee-um), meaning "one-zero-nine."

| 271 **Uun** ununnilium 110 | **ununnilium** *symbol: Uun • atomic number: 110 • period 7* |

Ununnilium (pronounced yoon-oon-nil-ee-um) was first made in 1994 by firing nickel ions into lead. A tiny number of ununnilium atoms were produced—in one experiment, just one atom was made in a week! Ununnilium is a temporary name that means "one-one-zero," but the name darmstadtium (chemical symbol Ds) was recommended in 2003, in honor of Darmstadt, where the element was first made.

| 272 **Uun** unununium 111 | **unununium** *symbol: Uuu • atomic number: 111 • period 7* |

Unununium was first made in 1994 at the Institute for Heavy Ion Research in Darmstadt by bombarding lead with bismuth ions. The temporary name unununium (pronounced yoon-oon-oon-ee-um) means "one-one-one."

| 285 **Uub** ununbium 112 | **ununbium** *symbol: Uub • atomic number: 112 • period 7* |

Scientists at the Institute for Heavy Ion Research in Germany produced ununbium in 1996 by bombarding lead with zinc ions. Ununbium (pronounced yoon-oon-by-um) is a temporary name that means "one-one-two." Because only very few atoms of ununbium have been produced, very little is known about its chemistry, and it has no practical uses so far.

The Ferromagnetic Metals

There are three transition metals that can be magnetized.
These are iron, cobalt, and nickel, and they are called
ferromagnetic metals. Alnico is an **alloy** of these three metals
and aluminum, and it makes very strong magnets. Iron,
cobalt, and nickel have many other uses, too.

56		**iron**
Fe		symbol: Fe • atomic number: 26 • period 4
iron		
26		

Iron is a shiny, light gray metal. Pure iron is quite soft, but
it becomes harder and stronger when it is alloyed with other
elements, such as carbon. Steel often contains less than
1 percent carbon, but cast iron, which is hard and **brittle,**
contains up to 4 percent carbon. Iron **reacts** with dilute
acids at room temperature, it reacts with oxygen in the air
when it is heated, and fine iron wool burns in air. Iron does
not react with water alone, but it rusts if it is exposed to
water and oxygen.

Our most important metal

Iron has been known for thousands of years, and it is our
most important metal. It is the fourth most abundant
element in Earth's crust, making up about 5 percent of it.
Iron is not found in its **native** state, except in some
meteorites, but it can be produced by just heating iron **ore**
with charcoal in a fire. Its name is from the Anglo-Saxon
word *iren,* and the symbol Fe comes from *ferrum,* the
Latin word for iron. Australia is the world's biggest
producer of iron ores, such as hematite
and magnetite, which both contain
forms of iron oxide. Iron is
produced from these ores by
heating them with carbon in
a blast furnace.

Magnetite is one of the ▶
most important ores of iron.
The other is hematite.

▲ *The rusting of this iron hull is speeded up by the presence of salt in seawater. A coat of paint keeps air and water away from the iron and prevents further rusting.*

Rusting

Rust is red-brown hydrated iron oxide. It easily flakes off to leave more iron exposed and, under the right conditions, iron objects may completely rust away. Rust spoils the appearance of cars, buildings, and equipment. It weakens joints and panels, and the damage it causes costs a lot of money to repair. Rusting is usually worse near the sea, because salt speeds up the process.

Iron will not rust if air or water cannot reach it. This is easily achieved by painting the metal, but it does not help if rusting has already started—the rust flakes off, taking the paint with it. Iron and steel can be coated in plastic or other metals, such as chromium, to stop rusting. "Tin" cans are made from steel coated with tin, and galvanized steel is coated with zinc. Because zinc is more reactive than iron, it continues to protect the iron even if it is scratched. If metal parts are going to move past each other, they are usually oiled or greased because paint would simply rub off.

The Blast Furnace, Iron, and Steel

Iron is **extracted** from iron **ore** in a huge steel column called a blast furnace that is lined with heat-resistant bricks to keep it from melting in the heat. The raw materials needed are iron ore, coke, limestone, and lots of hot air.

Hot air
The blast furnace needs to be really hot to get the **reactions** going inside it. The fuel used to do this is coke, a type of nearly pure carbon made from coal. It reacts with the oxygen in hot air that is blown into the bottom of the blast furnace, eventually increasing the temperature to about 2,912 °F (1,600 °C).

Carbon is more reactive than iron, so it can react with iron oxide and remove the oxygen from it if the temperature is high enough. However, carbon monoxide gas actually does this job in the blast furnace. When the coke burns, it produces carbon dioxide. This reacts with more coke to make carbon monoxide gas.

Getting iron from the ore
The hot carbon monoxide gas reacts with the iron oxide in the iron ore. This reaction produces carbon dioxide, iron, and a little more heat. The blast furnace is so hot that the iron melts and trickles down to the bottom.

The molten iron contains sandy impurities that must be removed before it is collected. Limestone contains calcium carbonate, and this breaks down in the heat of the blast furnace to form calcium oxide and carbon dioxide. The calcium oxide then reacts with the sand, which is mostly silica, to make a slag of calcium silicate. The slag floats on top of the molten iron and is collected separately.

The Crystal Palace *built for the Great Exhibition of 1851 in London was built from 3,500 tons of cast iron and 550 tons of wrought iron, and contained 300,000 panes of glass. It enclosed 1.3 million cubic yards (nearly a million cubic meters), yet took just nine months to build!* ▶

Casting the iron

The molten iron contains up to 4 percent carbon and other impurities, and some of it is allowed to cool in molds to produce cast iron. The Victorians in the 19th century used cast iron for all sorts of things, including ships, bridges, and buildings. It is hard but **brittle,** so today it is used for less demanding jobs, such as manhole covers and railings. Wrought iron is a tough and **malleable** form of iron that is used for forging objects. However, most iron is processed further to make steel.

Making steel

To convert iron into steel, various nonmetal impurities including carbon must be removed or **reduced.** Molten iron from the blast furnace is mixed with scrap iron, and pure oxygen is blown into the mixture. Carbon is oxidized to carbon monoxide gas that bubbles out of the molten iron. Silicon is oxidized to silica, and phosphorus is oxidized to phosphate. These impurities, together with sulfur, are removed by adding calcium oxide, which reacts with them and forms a slag. Other elements, including chromium, nickel, and manganese, are added to the steel to produce **alloys** such as stainless steel.

Uses of Iron

Iron is an important **mineral** in our diet. A person weighing 110 lb (50 kg) contains about 0.106 oz (3 g) of iron, nearly all of it in his or her red blood cells. These cells contain hemoglobin, the protein that carries oxygen in the blood. There is an iron **atom** at the heart of each hemoglobin **molecule.** If we do not get enough iron in our diet, we may suffer from anemia. People with anemia have pale skin and become breathless and dizzy because they are not getting enough oxygen to their cells. Iron (II) sulfate is used in tablets to help people who have anemia.

Iron and steel

Steel, and concrete reinforced with steel, is widely used in the construction of buildings and bridges. Most modern buildings have a framework of steel girders that takes the weight of the building. Without steel, buildings made just from brick or stone would need increasingly thicker walls at the bottom, which would limit their height. Steel is used to make railway lines, vehicles, and ships, as well as all sorts of machines and tools. Around 800 million tons of steel are used each year, or about 276 lb (125 kg) for each person in the world!

Steel is strong enough for us to build very large buildings, ships, and bridges, like this one over the River Tagus, near Lisbon in Portugal.

Magnets and motors

Electromagnets are made by passing electricity through a coil of wire. If the wire is wrapped around an iron core, the electromagnet becomes much stronger. Magnets made from iron and iron **compounds,** such as barium ferrite, are used in electric motors, generators, and television tubes. Videotapes and computer disks rely on magnetic fields to store their data, and they are coated with tiny particles of iron oxide.

Earth's core contains iron and nickel, and movements in it produce Earth's magnetic field. This is important to life on Earth because it stops the Sun's dangerous **radiation** from reaching the ground. Compasses made from magnetized iron rely on Earth's magnetic field to point to the north. However, compasses in steel ships may cause a problem. This is because they are likely to point to the ship's hull instead.

◀ This binnacle houses a ship's compass. It contains pieces of metal that can be adjusted to make sure that the compass points to north correctly.

Catalysts and color

Ammonia is used to make fertilizers and explosives. It is made by reacting nitrogen and hydrogen in a process called the Haber process, and iron is the **catalyst** that speeds up the **reaction.** Firework sparklers flash when burned in air because they contain iron filings.

Iron (III) oxide is red, and when it is very finely powdered, it is used in cosmetics. It is also used in "jewelers' rouge," used to gently polish jewelry and precious stones. Prussian Blue is a deep blue solid used in paints. It is formed when iron (III) chloride reacts with another iron compound called potassium hexacyanoferrate (II).

Cobalt

59 Co cobalt 27	cobalt
	symbol: Co • atomic number: 27 • period 4

Cobalt is a silvery-gray metal that is hard but **malleable.** It does not **react** with oxygen in the air unless it is heated. Cobalt does not react with water, but it will react with steam to produce cobalt oxide when it is heated, and it reacts slowly with acids. Cobalt is one of the three metals that can be made into magnets. The other two "ferromagnetic" metals, iron and nickel, are found on the left and right of cobalt in the **periodic table.**

Minerals containing cobalt have been used for thousands of years to make blue pottery and glass. However, cobalt itself was not discovered until 1735, when Georg Brandt, a Swedish chemist, studied the **ores** used to make blue glass. These were thought to contain bismuth, but by 1739, Brandt was able to isolate a new metal. He called this new metal cobalt, after the name of a mythical German goblin. Cobalt ores often contain arsenic, making them poisonous. The arsenic made the miners ill, and German miners believed that an evil goblin called the Kobold put these ores in the mines.

Cobalt is not found naturally as the free metal, and it makes up just 0.002 percent of Earth's crust. Several **minerals** contain cobalt, including linnaeite (cobalt sulfide) and cobaltite (cobalt arsenic sulfide). About 36 thousand tons of cobalt ores are mined each year, mostly in Africa and Canada, and cobalt is also **extracted** from wastes produced as by-products of the nickel and copper industry.

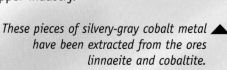

These pieces of silvery-gray cobalt metal ▲
have been extracted from the ores
linnaeite and cobaltite.

Around 20 thousand tons of cobalt are produced each year. Several methods are used to extract cobalt. In one method, the cobalt ore is heated strongly in air over several hours to produce cobalt sulfate. This is dissolved, and cobalt metal is then produced from it using **electrolysis.**

One of the major uses of cobalt is in the manufacture of permanent magnets (familiar, everyday magnets—not electromagnets). Cobalt is mixed with other metals to produce **alloys** such as alnico, which contains iron, aluminum, nickel, and cobalt. Alnico is used to make very strong magnets that keep their magnetism at high temperatures. Alnico magnets are the most widely used permanent magnets and are found in devices such as loudspeakers, microphones, and electric guitar pickups. Cobalt is used in "superalloys" that remain strong even at the high temperatures found in jet engines. It is also used as a **catalyst** for several industrial processes, including removing sulfur from crude oil and in the manufacture of plastics and fibers.

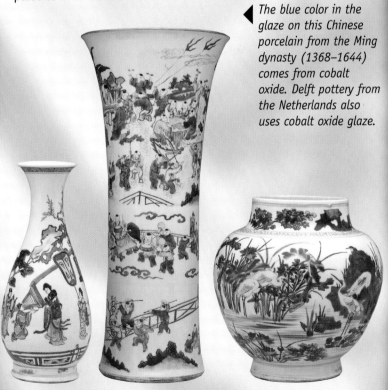

The blue color in the glaze on this Chinese porcelain from the Ming dynasty (1368–1644) comes from cobalt oxide. Delft pottery from the Netherlands also uses cobalt oxide glaze.

Uses of Cobalt

Radioactive cobalt

Isotopes are **atoms** of an **element** with the same number of **protons** and **electrons,** but different numbers of **neutrons.** Natural cobalt is made entirely of one isotope, cobalt-59, but scientists have been able to produce other isotopes artificially. One of them, cobalt-60, is very **radioactive.** This means that its **nucleus** can break apart and give off **radiation.** Cobalt-60 produces gamma radiation, a powerful form of invisible light.

Each **molecule** of vitamin B_{12} contains a cobalt atom. Vitamin B_{12} is found in milk, meat, and fish, and our bodies need it to make red blood cells. Some people have difficulty absorbing vitamin B_{12} and they may suffer from anemia as a result. To help with their diagnosis, doctors may ask these patients to swallow a small amount of vitamin B_{12} containing radioactive cobalt. The cobalt acts as a **tracer,** letting the doctor find out where the vitamin goes in the patient. There are other uses for radioactive cobalt, too.

The gamma radiation from cobalt-60 is used to sterilize medical equipment for use in operations, and to treat cancer by aiming it at cancerous cells. Engineers use it to inspect metal parts such as jet engine blades. It works a bit like a very powerful X-ray photograph, except that it shows cracks in the metal rather than broken bones.

In some countries, food is irradiated with gamma rays from cobalt-60 to preserve it. Irradiated food does not become radioactive, but it is often labeled with this international symbol, called the radura. Irradiated food is totally banned in Australia.

Cobalt compounds

Camcorders and laptop computers need lightweight batteries to power them. Nickel–cadmium (Ni–Cd, or nicad) batteries are often used, but a lithium-**ion** battery of the same size can store up to three times as much energy. Lithium cobalt oxide is used to make the **cathode** in lithium-ion batteries, thus avoiding the use of cadmium, a poisonous metal. However, the high cost of cobalt makes lithium-ion batteries much more expensive than nicad batteries.

Various cobalt **compounds,** including a black cobalt oxide, Co_3O_4, and pink cobalt carbonate, are used in glazes for pottery and **ceramics.** When the pottery is fired in the kiln, these compounds **decompose** or break down to form cobalt (II) oxide, CoO, with a deep blue color.

Detecting water

Paper containing cobalt chloride is often used to detect water in laboratory chemicals. It turns deep blue when it is dried in an oven, but turns pink when it is dipped into a substance containing water. Biologists also make use of this **reaction** when they are studying respiration in living things. Respiration is the chemical reaction that releases energy from food, and it happens in all living cells. When you breathe out, your breath contains water vapor, some of which is produced by respiration. If you breathe on a piece of blue cobalt chloride paper, it gradually turns pink because of its reaction with the water vapor in your breath.

◀ Cobalt chloride paper is used to test for water. It is blue when it is dry, but pink when it is damp.

Nickel

59		**nickel**
Ni		*symbol: Ni • atomic number: 28 • period 4*
nickel		
28		

Nickel is a hard but **malleable** silvery metal. Powdered nickel **reacts** with oxygen in the air, but lumps of the metal will usually react only when heated. Although it does not react with water or alkalis, nickel reacts with acids to produce colored nickel salts and hydrogen.

*Nickel is used as an industrial **catalyst** and to add **corrosion** resistance and strength to steel.* ▶

Minerals containing nickel have been used for hundreds of years to make green glass. However, nickel itself was not discovered until 1751, when Swedish chemist Axel Cronstedt studied one of the **ores** used to make green glass. He dissolved the ore in acid to make a green solution, then warmed it to leave green crystals behind. He produced an impure white metal from these crystals by heating them with carbon. Cronstedt called this metal nickel, after the name of the ore. The ore is now called nickeline, but was originally called kupfernickel, meaning "devil's copper." This was because, although it looked similar to copper ore, the miners were unable to get any copper out of it, and they believed that the devil was the cause!

Nickel is not found naturally as the free metal, but it makes up 0.007 percent of Earth's crust and about 4 percent of Earth's core. Luckily, nickel is found in many minerals around the world, so it is not necessary to drill down nearly 1,860 mi (3,000 km) to Earth's core! The main ores are pentlandite (nickel sulfide) and nickeline (nickel arsenide). Russia, Canada, and Australia are the main producers, but nickel ores are mined in over twenty countries, and about 1.25 million tons of nickel are produced each year.

The nickel ores are crushed and concentrated, then processed to remove some impurities and iron. The impure nickel is reacted with sulfuric acid to make a solution of nickel sulfate. When electricity is passed through this solution, pure nickel forms on the negative **electrode.**

Nickel sulfate is used as a **mordant,** meaning that it helps dyes stick to textiles. Nickel oxide is used to make the **cathodes** in rechargeable nickel–cadmium batteries, as well as in powerful, long-lasting nickel metal hydride batteries.

Nickel **compounds** must be handled carefully because they are poisonous, while nickel and its **alloys** can cause allergic skin rashes in some people.

▼ These familiar items are made from stainless steel that resists rusting. About 65 percent of all nickel is used in making stainless steel.

Uses of Nickel

Nickel and margarine

Nickel is used as a **catalyst** in the manufacture of margarine from vegetable oils. These oils are runny at room temperature, but when they are **reacted** with hydrogen using a nickel catalyst, their melting point increases and they become harder at room temperature. This is what it means when the ingredients include "hydrogenated vegetable oil."

Nickel plating

Nickel is coated onto other metals to protect them from rusting, usually by a process called **electroplating.** This involves passing electricity through a bath containing solutions of nickel chloride or nickel nitrate. However, nickel is usually mixed with other metals to form **alloys.**

Nickel alloys

The nickel coin is made from a silvery alloy containing 25 percent nickel and 75 percent copper. Similar alloys are used in European euro (€) coins. The €2 coin has an inner circle made from nickel covered by an alloy containing 75 percent copper, 20 percent zinc, and 5 percent nickel. This is surrounded by a ring made from the alloy used in the nickel coin. However, the biggest use for nickel is in making stainless steel.

The nickel and ▶ these euro coins contain an alloy of nickel and copper that looks shiny white.

Stainless steel mainly contains iron, chromium, and nickel. Types containing between 8 percent and 14 percent nickel are easy to clean, so they are widely used to make kitchen sinks, counters, and food processing equipment. Stronger stainless steel that resists **corrosion** very well contains less than about 7 percent nickel. These are used where salt water is involved, such as in equipment to produce fresh water from seawater. Nickel is also found in many other alloys, including heat-resistant "superalloys" used in jet engines.

Most materials expand when they are heated, and some expand more than others. Invar is an iron–nickel alloy containing 36 percent nickel. It expands ten times less than iron when it is heated. By altering its composition, its expansion can be made to match other materials. This makes it useful for keeping a gas-tight seal between the glass and metal in electric light bulbs, since both materials expand by the same amount when the bulb warms up.

A flexible alloy

Nitinol is an alloy consisting of 55 percent nickel and 45 percent titanium. William Buehler, an American metallurgist, discovered it in 1958. He named it after the symbols of the two metals in it, combined with the initial letters of the Naval Ordnance Laboratory where he worked. If an object made from Nitinol is bent, it goes back to its original shape when it is warmed. This makes the alloy very useful for making glasses frames and some surgical instruments. It is also very springy, so it is used in antennas for cell phones.

▼ *Glasses frames made from Nitinol spring back into shape after being bent.*

Group 11: The Coinage Metals

Because they are relatively unreactive, the metals in the eleventh **group,** copper, silver, and gold, have traditionally been used to make coins.

64 **Cu** copper 29	**copper** *symbol: Cu • atomic number: 29 • period 4*

Copper is a **malleable** metal with a distinctive orange-brown color. It does not **react** with oxygen in the air unless it is heated strongly, and it does not react with water or steam. The acids you use at school will not react with copper, but concentrated nitric acid attacks it, forming brown fumes of nitrogen oxide during the reaction.

Copper on its own is too soft to be very useful for tools and weapons, so it is usually mixed with other metals to form **alloys.** Bronze is an alloy of copper and tin that is much harder than copper alone. The Bronze Age began about 6,000 years ago when people learned how to make this substance. The Romans got most of their copper from the island of Cyprus, and the metal's name comes from the Latin word for Cyprus.

Copper has been known for thousands of years. It can be found in its **native** state as the free metal, but copper is also easy to **extract** from its **ores.** This is because it is fairly unreactive, so very little energy is needed to produce copper from its **compounds.** Thirteen million tons of copper are produced in the world each year, mostly from ores such as chalcopyrite, (copper iron sulfide) and cuprite (copper oxide).

Although copper can be found in its it is only rarely found like this now. All the best ores have already been mined, and most copper ores contai less than 2 percent copper.

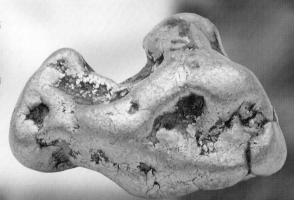

This is a natural nugget or lump of copper metal. ▶

Therefore, there is a lot of waste rock to be removed before the copper can be extracted, and a process called flotation separation is used to do this. The copper ore is crushed to a fine powder and mixed with water. Then lots of air is bubbled through it. The unwanted rock sinks to the bottom, while a froth containing copper compounds forms at the surface. The froth is concentrated and dried, and it is often mixed with scrap copper before being processed by roasting it in air. The copper is then purified using **electrolysis.**

It is possible that Neolithic people isolated copper by accident when they surrounded their cooking fires with colorful lumps of copper ore, such as green malachite (copper carbonate).
In the heat of the fire, the copper carbonate would easily ***decompose,*** *or break down, to form black copper (II) oxide:*

$$\text{copper carbonate} \xrightarrow{\text{heat}} \text{copper oxide + carbonate dioxide}$$
$$CuCO_3(s) \rightarrow CuO(s) + CO_2(g)$$

Carbon in the fuel would then reduce the copper oxide to shiny copper metal:

$$\text{copper (II) oxide + carbon} \rightarrow \text{copper + carbon dioxide}$$
$$2CuO(s) + C(s) \rightarrow 2Cu(s) + CO_2(g)$$

Carbon is more reactive than copper, so it can remove the oxygen from copper oxide.

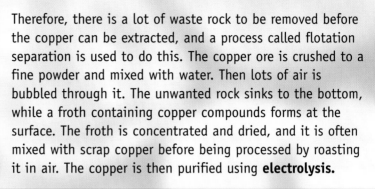

◀ *The Statue of Liberty in New York is made from a skin of copper sheeting riveted onto a steel frame. As the copper weathers and reacts with gases in the atmosphere, a protective green patina containing basic copper carbonate and basic copper sulfate forms on its surface.*

Uses of Copper

Copper against disease

Arthritis is a painful disease in which joints become swollen and difficult to move. Many people with arthritis wear copper bracelets because they believe that the copper eases the symptoms of the disease, but there is no scientific evidence showing this.

Legionnaire's disease is a serious lung disease that kills up to a fifth of the people who get it. It is caused by a bacterium called *Legionella pneumophila,* that is spread by contaminated water droplets from air conditioning systems. These systems may contain devices that release copper **ions** and silver ions into the water, killing the harmful bacteria.

Copper metal and its alloys

Copper is the second best conductor of electricity after silver, but it is about one hundred times cheaper, so it is widely used in the electrical and electronics industries. It is used in some radiators to carry away waste heat because it is also a good heat conductor, and the plumbing industry uses it for pipes and fittings because it does not react with water.

Since it is quite unreactive, copper is used on its own or mixed with other metals to make **alloys** that stay shiny. Nickel silver, an alloy of copper, zinc, and nickel, is used to make costume jewelry and "silver" coins. Screws, propellers, and musical instruments such as trumpets are often made from brass (an alloy of copper and zinc), while statues, bells, and coins are often made from bronze (a copper–tin alloy). Special tools that can be used without causing accidental sparks are made from beryllium–copper alloys. These kinds of non-sparking tools are needed in dusty factories, where a stray spark could cause an explosion.

Copper compounds

Copper (II) oxide, CuO, is used to make blue or green glazes for pottery. Copper nitrate is added to the gunpowder in fireworks to make the flame burn with a blue-green color.

Copper sulfate is needed during the **refining** of copper itself, but its main use is in agriculture. It is an ingredient of wood preservatives and **fungicides** such as "Bordeaux mixture," the traditional treatment for grapes used for wine-making.

Food tests

Some sugars, such as glucose and fructose, can **react** with copper sulfate solution under the right conditions. These sugars are called **reducing** sugars, and they can be detected using a mixture called Benedict's reagent. This contains sodium citrate and sodium carbonate in addition to copper sulfate. It is a clear blue solution, but if it is mixed with these sugars and warmed up, it forms a **precipitate** of solid red copper (I) oxide, Cu_2O. A similar change happens when Fehling's solution, which also contains copper sulfate, is heated with these sugars.

Proteins can be detected using the Biuret test. The test substance is mixed with sodium hydroxide solution, and then some copper sulfate solution is added. If there is any protein in the test substance, the mixture turns purple.

Copper is a good, relatively cheap conductor of heat that does not react with water. It is ideal for use in central heating systems.

Silver

108	
Ag	**silver**
silver	symbol: Ag • atomic number: 47 • period 5
47	

Silver is a shiny white metal. It is quite unreactive, and does not **react** with air or water unless they are contaminated with **corrosive** chemicals such as hydrogen sulfide. Silver does not react with dilute acids, but it will react with concentrated sulfuric and nitric acids, especially when it is heated.

Silver has been known for thousands of years, and it has been widely used for coins, jewelry, and expensive ornaments. The Romans used silver coins, and the symbol for silver comes from the Latin word "argentum," meaning silver. Its name comes from the Anglo-Saxon word for silver.

Silver makes up a tiny proportion of Earth's crust, and on average there is less than a gram (0.035 ounce) of it in every 20 tons of rock. However, it can be found as the free metal and in many **minerals.** The most important silver **ore** is acanthite, also called argentite, that contains silver sulfide. Minerals that contain copper, lead, or zinc sulfides usually contain small amounts of silver. Galena, or lead sulfide, is one of the most important sources of silver—it can contain up to 1 percent silver. About three-quarters of the silver produced comes from the wastes left behind after **refining** copper, lead, or zinc.

Mexico, Peru, the United States, Australia, and Canada are the major sources of silver, and about 18,000 tons of silver are produced in the world each year. Depending on the starting material, different methods are used to **extract** it, and all involve several complex steps to produce pure silver.

*▶ **Native** silver (twisted, wirelike formations) is usually found as a **compound** in minerals such as argentite and horn silver, although it may be found alone, as on this rock.*

▲ American Eagle silver dollar coins, like this one, are 1.57 in. (4 cm) in diameter and are made from 99.9 percent silver.

Money, money, money

Silver has been used to make coins since Roman times. However, the value of the silver in coins has become greater than the face value of the coins themselves. Modern "silver" coins often use a copper–nickel **alloy** that has a silvery appearance. If these coins were made from the same mass of silver, the metal itself would be worth over 20 times the face value of the coin!

Silver coins are still made, but mostly for investors who want to put their savings into buying valuable metals. Silver **bullion** bars are also sold. On its own, silver scratches easily, so copper is usually added to it to make it harder. American Eagle coins are made from a silver–copper alloy containing just 0.07 percent copper, and British Britannia coins are made from Britannia silver, which is 95.8 percent silver. However, both coins contain 1 troy oz (31.1 g) of silver.

Silver–copper alloys are also used in jewelry. You can choose from different jewelry alloys, depending on how much money you have to spend. Sterling silver contains 92.5 percent silver, and costs more than jewelry silver, which contains only 80 percent silver.

Uses of Silver

Silver is the best conductor of electricity. It is widely used on its own, or **alloyed** with palladium or zinc, in printed circuit boards and electrical contacts. Metal parts are often joined together using silver solders—alloys of silver, copper, and zinc. Silver is a relatively poor **catalyst** compared to the other transition metals. However, it is ideal for controlling the potentially explosive **reaction** that the chemical industry uses to produce a substance called epoxyethane. This is an important **compound** that is used to make car antifreeze, polyesters, and detergents. Some silver compounds are very important, too.

Chemical testing

Silver nitrate dissolves in water, unlike most other silver compounds. Chemists use silver nitrate solution to test their chemicals to see if there are any chlorides, such as sodium chloride, dissolved in them. Silver nitrate reacts with chlorides to produce white silver chloride. This does not dissolve in water, so it forms a cloudy white **precipitate.**

The equation for using silver nitrate solution to find out if a liquid contains dissolved sodium chloride (common salt) is:

silver + sodium → sodium + silver
nitrate chloride nitrate chloride

$$AgNO_3(aq) + NaCl(aq) \rightarrow NaNO_3(aq) + AgCl(s)$$

Sodium nitrate dissolves in water, so you do not see it, but silver chloride forms a cloudy white precipitate because it does not dissolve in water. Chemists usually add a little nitric acid before they add the silver nitrate solution.

Silver nitrate solution can also be used to test for bromides and iodides. Bromides produce a cream colored precipitate with silver nitrate, and iodides produce a yellow precipitate.

Photography

Silver chloride, bromide, and iodide gradually turn black if they are left in the light. This is because the light causes them to **decompose** or break down to form tiny particles of silver that look black. An English scientist named William Talbot discovered how to make photographs using this reaction in the early part of the 19th century. Talbot coated some paper with silver chloride, covered it with an object such as a leaf, and then exposed it to light. Where the paper was exposed to the light, the silver chloride turned black, but where it was covered up, it stayed white.

Talbot patented his method in 1841, but photography has developed considerably since then. Many advances have been made in the chemistry of photography, but it remains the biggest single use for silver. Silver chloride, silver bromide, and silver iodide are all used in photographic printing papers and films. However, as digital photography becomes more important, the demand for silver for photography is likely to go down.

◀ *This photograph was made using William Talbot's talbotype (calotype) method, using silver salts.*

Batteries

Silver (I) oxide, with a little manganese (IV) oxide and graphite added to conduct electricity, is used to make the **cathode** in silver-zinc batteries. These produce a lot of energy for their mass, so they are widely used in spacecraft, cameras, watches, and so on.

◀ *These small "button" batteries contain silver oxide. They are used to power watches, calculators, and cameras.*

Gold

197 **Au** gold 79	**gold** *symbol: Au • atomic number: 79 • period 6*

Gold is a dense metal with a distinctive rich yellow color. It does not **react** with air, water, or steam, but it will react with chlorine. The acids you use at school will not react with gold, but a mixture of hydrochloric acid and concentrated nitric acid, called **aqua regia,** will dissolve gold.

Gold is very rare, making up just a small 0.000 0003 percent of Earth's crust. However, it can be found in its natural state as the free metal, and it is often already very pure. As a result, gold has been known and valued highly for thousands of years. Medieval alchemists spent fruitless centuries trying to turn lead into gold, and wars have been started and civilizations have fallen to satisfy the desire for the shiny, unreactive metal.

Gold rush!

Pieces of gold can be washed out of rocks into rivers and streams. These nuggets can be isolated by panning. Some material from the riverbed is scooped into a shallow dish, then swirled gently in the water. Gold is very **dense,** so it stays in the bottom of the pan while the less dense sand and pebbles are washed out. Of course, there needs to be enough gold in the riverbed to make panning worthwhile! In the California Gold Rush of 1849, a quarter of a million people eventually headed west to try to make their fortune, but only a few became rich.

Gold has been highly prized for thousands of years. This statue of Buddha was crafted hundreds of years ago. ▶

▲ *Nuggets of gold are often found in streams and riverbeds where the rain has washed them out of the rocks.*

About 1,500 tons of gold are produced in the world each year, mainly in South Africa. There are some **minerals** that contain gold, such as calaverite (gold telluride), but most gold is found in its **native** form mixed with rock. The gold is **extracted** using two main methods.

Mercury can dissolve many other metals to form **alloys** called **amalgams.** When minerals containing gold are mixed with mercury, the gold dissolves to form an amalgam. This is filtered to remove the undissolved impurities. The amalgam is then heated to drive off the mercury, leaving purified gold behind.

In the second method, the minerals are added to sodium cyanide solution. This reacts with the gold to make sodium cyanoaurite solution, a gold **compound.** The solution is then filtered to remove the undissolved impurities. When zinc powder is added, it reacts with the sodium cyanoaurite to produce solid gold.

Gold is able to form a few compounds even though it is very unreactive. Potassium cyanoaurite is used for gold-plating metal objects using electricity, and some photographers use chlorauric acid to adjust the appearance of their photographs. People with inflamed joints caused by arthritis may get some relief from pain if they receive regular injections of a gold compound called sodium aurothiomalate.

Uses of Gold

The biggest industrial use of gold is in the manufacture of electronic equipment. It is nearly as good as copper at conducting electricity, but is less reactive and does not tarnish at all, so it is used to make electrical contacts and fine wires to connect computer chips. Also, if you have failed to look after your teeth properly (and if you have plenty of money) you might decide to get a gold filling. These are soft enough not to wear away the other teeth, they do not chip or tarnish, and they give you a flashy smile!

▲ Visors on space suits worn by astronauts have a thin layer of gold to reflect infrared **radiation**.

Gold reserves

Gold is a very expensive metal because it is so rare. Pure gold is too soft for most purposes, so it is often **alloyed** with other metals, such as silver and copper. The proportion of gold in an alloy is measured in **karats:** pure gold is 24 karat gold, while an alloy containing 50 percent gold is 12 karat gold. The cheapest jewelry gold is usually 9 karat gold, but more expensive jewelry gold, such as 18 karat gold, is also popular. Coinage gold usually contains a small amount of silver, but the amount varies from country to country. British Sovereigns and American Eagles are 22 karat gold (91.67 percent gold), but Canadian Maple Leafs are made with "Four Nines" gold that is 99.99 percent gold! The price of gold varies, but typically a coin that contains 1 troy ounce (31.1 grams of gold) costs hundreds of euros or dollars.

For wealthy people and governments, gold can be stored and traded as **bullion** bars. The "London Good Delivery Bar" is the size usually stored by central banks, and it weighs 12.5 kg (27.56 lb)! Huge amounts of gold are stored by governments in their "gold reserves," including over 8,000 tons in the United States alone.

Thin gold

Gold is extremely **ductile** and **malleable.** Just 1 g (0.0027 oz) of it could be stretched into a wire over 1.24 mi (2 km) long, and it can be hammered into sheets just 0.0008 in. (0.02 mm) thick! This gold leaf, as it is known, is used to decorate books, fine art, and furniture. Gold is a very good heat reflector, so satellites and space probes are often coated with it to protect them while in space. Astronauts' visors and the glass in some buildings are also examples of the use of gold as a heat reflector.

Group 12: Zinc, Cadmium, and Mercury

The last group contains zinc, cadmium, and mercury. Although they are usually included in the transition metals, their d subshells are completely filled with **electrons,** so they do not behave as transition metals at all.

65 **Zn** zinc 30	**zinc** *symbol: Zn • atomic number: 30 • period 4*

Zinc is a blue-white metal that is **brittle** at room temperature but becomes easier to work with above 212 °F (100 °C). It **reacts** with acids but does not react with water. Zinc reacts with the oxygen in damp air, gradually turning gray-black, and it burns in air to produce zinc oxide when it is heated.

Zinc was first recognized as an **element** in 1789 by the French chemist Antoine Lavoisier. He wrote an important book called *Traité Élementaire de Chimie,* in which he listed the elements known at the time. Lavoisier did not get it all correct, though—he included light and heat in his list! However, people had known about zinc and its **compounds** for thousands of years before then.

▲

These pieces of pure zinc are extracted from the ores sphalerite or zinc blende (zinc sulfide) and smithsonite (zinc carbonate).

Calamine and brass

Calamine (zinc carbonate) was used by the Romans to cure skin diseases. They also made brass, an **alloy** of zinc and copper, by heating charcoal, zinc carbonate, and copper together. It is very difficult to **extract** zinc from its **ores,** but by the 14th century, thousands of tons of zinc were being produced in India. In 1743, William Champion started the first commercial European production of zinc at Bristol in England.

Zinc is the 23rd most abundant element in Earth's crust, making up about 0.007 percent of it. Although zinc is not found naturally as the free metal, it is found all over the world in several **minerals.** The main kinds of zinc ores are zinc blende and sphalerite (zinc sulfide), and smithsonite (zinc carbonate). Ores containing about nine million tons of zinc are mined each year, mainly in Australia and China. The United States and Canada also produce significant amounts.

There are two main ways to extract zinc, and in each case the zinc ores are first roasted in air to produce zinc oxide.

The equation for the production of zinc oxide from zinc sulfide ore is:

zinc sulfide + oxygen → zinc oxide + sulfur dioxide
$$2ZnS(s) + 3O_2(g) \rightarrow 2ZnO(s) + 2SO_2(g)$$

The sulfur dioxide produced in the reaction is used to make sulfuric acid.

If the zinc is going to be extracted by **electrolysis,** the zinc oxide is reacted with sulfuric acid to produce a solution of zinc sulfate. When electricity is passed through this, pure zinc metal forms at the negative **electrode.**

The second method involves heating the zinc oxide in a furnace with coke, a cheap form of nearly pure carbon. This produces carbon dioxide and impure zinc metal. Zinc has a low boiling point for a metal, 1,664.6 °F (907 °C), so it can be purified by distillation. The impure zinc is heated until it turns into a gas. This is separated from the impurities, and then cooled and solidified.

Uses of Zinc

Musical instruments such as the alto saxophone shown here are made from brass, an alloy of zinc and copper.

Zinc is widely used to coat other metals, such as steel. This is called galvanizing, and it is so important that about half of all the zinc produced is used in this way. Zinc melts at just 788 °F (420 °C), so steel is easily galvanized just by dipping it into a bath of molten zinc. Because zinc is more **reactive** than iron, it **corrodes** before the iron in the steel does. This is called **sacrificial protection** because the zinc "sacrifices" itself to save the steel. The steel is protected even if the layer of zinc is scratched, so galvanized steel has a huge number of uses, including cars, buildings, bridges, and roofs.

Zinc alloys

Brass, an **alloy** containing copper and 20 percent to 45 percent zinc, is the oldest zinc alloy. It is easily worked into shape but harder than copper on its own. It does not rust and it conducts electricity well. Brass is used to make electrical and plumbing fittings, screws, equipment for boats, and scientific instruments such as telescopes.

Zinc and aluminum form a strong alloy with a low melting point. This allows it to be molded into complex shapes in a process called diecasting. Diecast objects are found in parts for cars, aircraft, and household appliances. When zinc and lead are mixed together, they produce alloys with low melting points. These are use as solders to join pipes and electrical components. Because relatively little heat is needed to melt the solder, the electrical components are not damaged when they are joined.

The first practical battery was the Leclanché cell, named after Georges Leclanché, the French engineer who invented it in 1866. It used zinc and carbon **electrodes.** Ordinary modern batteries, including many alkaline batteries, also use zinc alloy electrodes.

Zinc compounds

Zinc oxide is a white powder used in lotions, bandages, and cosmetics because it helps to soothe and heal damaged skin. When you were a baby, your bottom was probably protected by a zinc oxide cream each time you had your diaper changed! Now that you are older, you are more likely to come across zinc oxide mixed with titanium (IV) oxide in sunblock preparations.

Zinc sulfide is a **phosphor,** meaning that it gives off light after being exposed to **radiation** or light. It is used in luminous paints, toys that glow in the dark, fluorescent lights, and television screens. When **radioactivity** was first discovered, scientists used a device called a spinthariscope to detect the radiation coming off radioactive substances. It consisted of a tube with the radioactive substance at one end and a screen coated with zinc sulfide at the other end. To measure how radioactive the substance was, the scientist counted the tiny flashes of light on the screen caused by the radiation.

◀ *When taking part in outdoor pursuits, it is advisable to wear sunblock on the exposed parts of your body to protect them from the Sun's harmful rays.*

Cadmium

112 **Cd** cadmium 48	**cadmium** *symbol: Cd • atomic number: 48 • period 5*

Cadmium is a silvery-white metal with a bluish tinge. It is soft and easily cut with a knife. The melting and boiling points of cadmium are quite low for a metal, and it produces a yellow vapor when heated. Cadmium is chemically very similar to zinc, which is just above it in the **periodic table.** It does not **react** with water or alkalis, but it reacts with hot acids, and it burns in air when heated to form brown cadmium oxide. The metal and its **compounds** are very poisonous, so they need to be handled with great care. Despite this, they have many uses, including the manufacture of batteries and television sets.

Cadmium was discovered in 1817 by the German chemist Friedrich Stromeyer. He studied a **mineral** that contained zinc carbonate. Zinc carbonate is white, and when it is heated, it **decomposes,** or breaks down, to form zinc oxide. This is yellow when it is hot, but it turns white when it cools down. However, the mineral that Stromeyer studied turned orange when it was heated, and it stayed that way. He decided that it must contain another metallic **element** besides zinc, and eventually he managed to isolate a previously unknown metal.

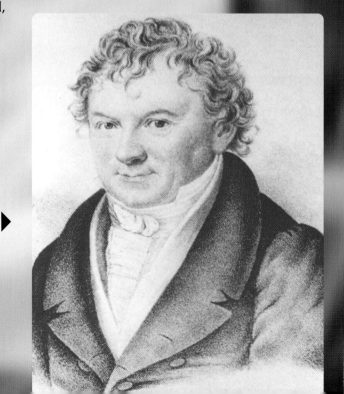

Friedrich Stromeyer, who discovered cadmium, named the new element after cadmia, the mineral from which it came.

About 1,800 tons of cadmium are produced in the world each year, but almost none of it comes from a cadmium **ore.** Cadmium makes up only just 0.000 02 percent of Earth's crust. It is not found naturally as the free metal, and cadmium ores are very rare. The only commercially valuable cadmium ore is greenockite, that contains cadmium sulfide. Greenockite is named after Lord Greenock, who owned the land in Scotland where it was first discovered.

The equations for producing cadmium from cadmium sulfide are:

cadmium + oxygen → cadmium + sulfur
sulfide   oxide   dioxide

$$2CdS(s) + 3O_2(g) \rightarrow 2CdO(s) + 2SO_2(g)$$

cadmium oxide + carbon → cadmium + carbon dioxide

$$2CdO(s) + C(s) \rightarrow 2Cd(s) + CO_2(g)$$

Zinc ores contain tiny amounts of cadmium, so most cadmium is **extracted** from the by-products of zinc **refining.** Zinc ores, such as sphalerite (zinc sulfide), are roasted in air to produce zinc oxide. This is then heated strongly with coke, which is mostly carbon, to produce zinc. If the original ore contained a little cadmium, this will be mixed with the zinc. The two metals have very different boiling points, so they can be separated from each other by distillation.

These are nuggets of pure cadmium. The metal is often associated with zinc ores such as sphalerite (zinc sulfide) and also occurs as the mineral greenockite (cadmium sulfide).

Uses of Cadmium

The surfaces of steel and aluminum coated with cadmium have a lower friction than the uncoated metals. This means that metal parts coated with cadmium can slide over each other more easily. As a result, some moving parts in cars and aircraft may be coated with cadmium. Cadmium also protects steel from rusting, just as zinc does.

▲ *Aircraft engine parts may be coated with cadmium to reduce the friction between moving parts and to resist rusting.*

Small amounts of cadmium metal are often mixed with other metals to make **alloys.** Copper alloyed with about 1 percent cadmium is twice as strong as copper on its own, and it is widely used for telephone cables and car radiators. Cadmium also lowers the melting point of some alloys. Woods metal is a very unusual alloy because it melts at just 158 °F (70 °C)—less than the temperature of a fresh cup of tea! It is made from a mixture of bismuth, lead, tin, and 12.5 percent cadmium. Woods metal is used in the valves of automatic sprinkler systems found in the ceilings of shops and factories. If there is a fire, the metal valve melts and releases water over the flames.

Pigments and plastics

Cadmium sulfide and cadmium selenium sulfide are used to make yellow, orange, and red **pigments** for artists' paints. Because they keep their colors at high temperatures, these pigments are often used in paints for the pipes in chemical factories, and in colored glass. Small amounts of cadmium pigments are added to plastics, including polyethylene and nylon, to make objects such as bright yellow gas pipes.

Polyvinyl chloride, PVC, gradually becomes **brittle** when it is exposed to the **ultraviolet light** in sunshine. To help prevent this damage, small amounts of chemicals called stabilizers are added to the plastic when it is being made. Cadmium stearate is frequently used as a stabilizer.

Electronics and batteries

Cadmium sulfide is used to make light-sensitive electronic devices, including solar cells, photocopier systems, and camera exposure meters. It is a **phosphor,** meaning that it gives off light when it is exposed to **radiation** such as **electron** beams, and it provides the green color in television pictures.

Nickel-cadmium batteries containing cadmium and cadmium hydroxide account for over two-thirds of the cadmium used. These batteries are often called nicads from Ni–Cd, the chemical symbols for nickel and cadmium. Rechargeable nicad batteries are widely used in cell phones, laptop computers, and other portable electrical equipment. Large industrial nicad batteries are used to supply emergency power in case of an electricity failure, and they are also used to power the starter motors for trains and aircraft.

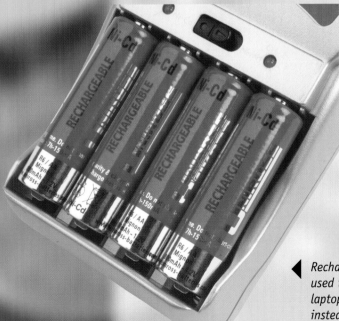

Rechargeable nicad batteries are used to power camcorders and laptop computers, and are used instead of ordinary batteries in toys.

Mercury

| 201 Hg mercury 80 | **mercury** symbol: Hg • atomic number: 80 • period 6 |

Mercury is a silvery metal with a very interesting property—it is the only metal that is liquid at room temperature. Because it is nearly fourteen times **denser** than water, metal objects will float on the surface of the liquid form. Mercury is highly poisonous to all living things, so great care must be taken when handling it.

Mercury does not **react** with water or hydrochloric acid, but it reacts with concentrated nitric acid and dissolves in boiling sulfuric acid. If it is heated above about 662 °F (350 °C), mercury reacts with oxygen in the air to form mercury oxide, a red solid. It dissolves most other metals to form special **alloys** called **amalgams.** Amalgam tooth fillings are made from mercury, silver, and tin.

Mercury has been known for thousands of years, since it is easily extracted from its main **ore**, cinnabar, simply by heating it in air. The cinnabar mines at Almadén in Spain have been in use for 6,000 years.

Quicksilver

Mercury is named after the Roman god Mercurius. It has also been known as quicksilver, meaning "alive silver." The chemical symbol Hg comes from *hydrargyrum,* Greek for "water silver." The Romans were well aware of its dangers, and condemned their prisoners to work in the cinnabar mines, where the poisonous metal would usually kill them within three years!

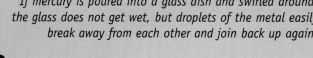

If mercury is poured into a glass dish and swirled around, the glass does not get wet, but droplets of the metal easily break away from each other and join back up again.

Mercury is quite rare in Earth's crust, only forming about 0.000 05 percent of it. However, there are more than 20 **minerals** that contain mercury, including cinnabar (mercury sulfide), and it is sometimes found in its **native** form as the free metal. About 1,400 tons of mercury are **extracted** in the world each year, and more than a third of this comes from Spain. To extract the mercury, crushed cinnabar is mixed with a stream of hot air. The oxygen in the air reacts with the sulfur in the cinnabar to form sulfur dioxide, and the mercury is released as mercury vapor. The vapor is removed and cooled so that it condenses to form liquid mercury metal.

Like most liquids, mercury expands when it is warmed. It does this in a regular way, allowing very accurate thermometers for measuring temperature to be made. At school you are more likely to use alcohol thermometers, because if a mercury thermometer is accidentally broken, special procedures are needed to make sure that no one is affected and that the poisonous metal is properly disposed of.

You are also not allowed to carry anything containing mercury onto an aircraft because aircraft are made from aluminum alloys. If any of the mercury escapes, it will dissolve the aluminum, making an amalgam and damaging the aircraft.

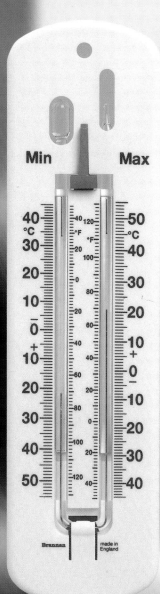

◀ *A German physicist named Gabriel Fahrenheit invented the alcohol thermometer in 1709 and the mercury thermometer five years later.*

Uses of Mercury

Barometers

Barometers measure atmospheric pressure. An Italian physicist named Evangelista Torricelli invented the mercury barometer in 1643 when he filled a long glass tube with mercury, then turned it upside down in a dish of mercury. He found that the mercury ran out of the tube until about 30 in. (760 mm) was left in it. The pressure of the air on the mercury in the dish pushed the mercury up the tube and kept it there.

If the air pressure goes down, so does the column of mercury in a barometer. Barometers can give you some warning of changes in the weather because different types of weather are associated with different air pressures. If the air pressure goes up, the weather is likely to be fine, but if it goes down, it is likely to bring rain.

Mercury compounds

Mercury (II) oxide, HgO, is a yellow-red solid that is used to make other mercury **compounds.** If it is heated, it easily breaks down to produce mercury and oxygen, a **reaction** that led to the discovery of oxygen by Joseph Priestley in 1774. Mercury oxide mixed with graphite is one of the **electrodes** in zinc–mercury oxide batteries, often used to power hearing aids. However, just like the metal itself, mercury compounds are very poisonous. They can cause birth defects and damage to the kidneys and brain.

Minamata disease

In 1956, fishermen and their families in the southern Japanese city of Minamata began to fall ill. They found it difficult to move properly, and suffered headaches and slurred speech. Thousands of people became ill, and many died. The cause turned out to be mercury poisoning from eating contaminated fish caught in Minamata Bay. A local chemical company used mercury as a **catalyst** to make ethanal, a raw material for making plastics. Unfortunately, methyl mercury was also made in the process. This chemical substance was discharged into the bay in waste water, and about 200 tons of mercury ended up in the sea. Once there, it built up in the food chain in larger and larger amounts in a process called bioaccumulation. Tiny animals and plants absorbed it and were then eaten by small fish. These fish became contaminated themselves, and were eaten by larger fish that absorbed even more methyl mercury. People eating the fish received the largest dose of mercury and became seriously ill as a result. After the cause was discovered, the bay was dredged to remove the contaminated sediment. Today, enough years have passed that it is now safe to eat fish caught there.

The people of Minamata protested against the dumping of waste mercury compounds into their bay. Many of them had suffered mercury poisoning after eating fish caught there.

Find out More About the Transition Metals

Elements

The table below contains some further information about the properties of the transition metals in this book. The artificial **elements** have been made only in tiny amounts, often only a few **atoms,** so very little is known about their properties.

Element	Symbol	Atomic number	Melting point °F/°C	Boiling point °F/°C
cadmium	Cd	48	609.8/321	1,410.8/766
cobalt	Co	27	2,723.0/1,495	5,198.0/2,870
copper	Cu	29	1,981.4/1,083	4,652.6/2,567
gold	Au	79	1,947.2/1,064	5,084.6/2,807
iridium	Ir	77	4,364.6/2,407	7,466.0/4,130
iron	Fe	26	2,796.8/1,536	4,982.0/2,750
mercury	Hg	80	−38.2/-39	674.6/357
nickel	Ni	28	2,647.4/1,453	4,949.6/2,732
osmium	Os	76	5,529.2/3,054	9,080.6/5,027
palladium	Pd	46	2,829.2/1,554	5,684.0/3,140
platinum	Pt	78	3,221.6/1,772	6,920.6/3,827
rhodium	Rh	45	3570.8/1,966	6,740.6/3,727
ruthenium	Ru	44	4,190.0/2,310	7,052.0/3,900
silver	Ag	47	1,763.6/962	4,013.6/2,212
zinc	Zn	30	788.0/420	1,664.6/907

The following elements can be found in *Tungsten, and the Elements of Groups 3 to 7.*

Element	Symbol	Element	Symbol
bohrium	Bh	scandium	Sc
chromium	Cr	seaborgium	Sg
dubnium	Db	tantalum	Ta
hafnium	Hf	technetium	Tc
manganese	Mn	titanium	Ti
molybdenum	Mo	tungsten	W
niobium	Nb	vanadium	V
rhenium	Re	yttrium	Y
rutherfordium	Rf	zirconium	Zr

Compounds

These tables show you the chemical formulas of a selection of the **compounds** mentioned in the book. For example, nickel sulfate has the formula $NiSO_4$. This means it is made from one nickel atom, one sulfur atom, and four oxygen atoms, joined together by chemical **bonds.**

Cadmium compound	formula
cadmium hydroxide	$Cd(OH)_2$
cadmium oxide	CdO
cadmium sulfide	CdS

Cadmium compounds

Cobalt compound	formula
cobalt (II) chloride	$CoCl_2$
cobalt oxide	Co_3O_4
cobalt (II) sulfate	$CoSO_4$
cobalt (II) sulfide	CoS
cobalt (II) oxide	CoO

Cobalt compounds

Copper compound	formula
copper (II) carbonate	$CuCO_3$
copper (II) chloride	$CuCl_2$
copper (II) sulfate	$CuSO_4$
copper (I) oxide (red)	Cu_2O
copper (II) oxide (black)	CuO

Copper compounds

Gold compound	formula
chlorauric acid	$HAuCl_4$
gold telluride	$AuTe_2$

Gold compounds

Iridium compound	formula
iridium (IV) oxide	IrO_2

Iridium compounds

Find out more continued

Iron compounds

Iron compound	formula
iron (II) chloride	$FeCl_2$
iron (III) chloride	$FeCl_3$
iron (III) oxide (hematite)	Fe_2O_3
magnetite	Fe_3O_4

Mercury compounds

Mercury compound	formula
mercury (II) oxide	HgO
mercury (II) sulfide	HgS

Nickel compounds

Nickel compound	formula
nickel (II) chloride	$NiCl_2$
nickel (II) oxide	NiO
nickel (II) sulfate	$NiSO_4$
nickel (II) sulfide	NiS

Osmium compounds

Osmium compound	formula
osmium (IV) oxide	OsO_2
osmium (VIII) oxide	OsO_4

Platinum compounds

Platinum compound	formula
platinum arsenide (sperrylite)	$PtAs_2$
cisplatin	$Pt(NH_3)_2Cl_2$

Silver compounds

Silver compound	formula
silver (I) nitrate	$AgNO_3$
silver (I) sulfide	Ag_2S
silver (I) oxide	Ag_2O

Zinc compounds

Zinc compound	formula
zinc oxide	ZnO
zinc sulfate	$ZnSO_4$
zinc sulfide	ZnS

Glossary

adsorb stick to a surface

alpha radiation (α radiation) waves of energy caused by quickly moving helium nuclei that have broken away from an unstable nucleus

alloy mixture of two or more metals, or mixture of a metal and a nonmetal

amalgam mixture formed when mercury dissolves another metal, such as gold

aqua regia mixture of concentrated nitric acid and hydrochloric acid that can dissolve gold and platinum

atom smallest particle of an element that has the properties of that element

atomic number number of protons in the nucleus of an atom

bond force that join atoms together

brittle likely to break into small pieces when hit

bullion precious metal, especially gold or silver, usually formed into bars

catalyst substance that speeds up reactions without getting used up

cathode electrode that can have a negative charge

ceramic tough solid made by heating clay and other substances to high temperatures in an oven. Plates, bathroom tiles, and toilet bowls are made from ceramics.

compound substance made from the atoms of two or more elements, joined together by chemical bonds

corrosion reaction of a metal with oxygen in the air. This forms a substance on the surface of the metal.

decay process in which the nucleus of a radioactive substance breaks up, giving off radiation and becoming the nucleus of another element

decompose to break down a compound into simpler substances, such as the elements that make it up

density mass of a substance compared to its volume. To find the density of a substance, you divide its mass by its volume.

ductile easily pulled into a thin wire

electrode solid that conducts electricity, such as graphite or a metal. Electrodes are found in batteries and are also used in electrolysis and electroplating.

electrolysis process of breaking down or decomposing a compound by passing electricity through it. The compound must be molten or dissolved in a liquid for electrolysis to work.

electron particle in an atom that has a negative electric charge. Electrons are found in shells around the nucleus of an atom

electroplating coating a metal with another metal using electricity

element substance made from only one type of atom

extract to remove a chemical from a mixture of chemicals

fungicide chemical that kills fungi

group vertical column of elements in the periodic table. Elements in a group have similar properties.

ion charged particle made when atoms lose or gain electrons.

isotope atoms of an element with the same number of protons and electrons, but a different number of neutrons. Isotopes share the same atomic number but they have a different mass number.

karat measure of the purity of gold. One karat is 1/24th or 4.17 percent, so 12 karat gold is 50 percent gold.

malleable able to be bent into shape without breaking

mass number in the nucleus of an atom, the number of protons added to the number of neutrons

mineral substance that is found naturally but does not come from animals or plants. Metal ores and limestone are examples of minerals.

molecule smallest particle of an element or compound that exists by itself. A molecule is made from two or more atoms joined together.

mordant chemical that helps a dye to stick to fabric fibers

native found as the pure metallic element, not combined in a compound

neutron particle in an atom's nucleus that does not have an electric charge

nucleus center part of an atom made from protons and neutrons that has a positive electric charge.

ore substance containing minerals from which metals are taken out and purified

period horizontal row of elements in the periodic table

periodic table table in which all the known elements are arranged into groups and periods

phosphor chemical that gives off light when it absorbs energy

pigment solid substance that gives color to a paint or other substance. Pigments do not dissolve in water.

precipitate solid that appears when two solutions are mixed

product substance made in a chemical reaction

proton particle in an atom's nucleus that has a positive electric charge

proton number see **atomic number**

radiation energy or particles given off when an atom decays

radioactive producing radiation

reaction chemical change that produces new substances

reduce to take away oxygen from an element or compound in a chemical reaction, or to add electrons

refining removing impurities from a substance to make it more pure. It can also mean separating the different substances in a mixture, for example, in oil refining.

sacrificial protection method used to stop iron and steel from rusting

subatomic particle particle smaller than an atom, such as a proton, neutron, or electron

tracer chemical that scientists can easily follow to see where it goes

ultraviolet light high-energy invisible light just beyond the blue end of the spectrum

volatile easily changed into a gas

Timeline

copper, gold, iron, mercury, and silver discovered	ancient times	
cobalt discovered	1735	Georg Brandt
platinum discovered	1735	Antonio de Ulloa
first commercial European production of zinc	1743	William Champion
nickel discovered	1751	Axel Cronstedt
osmium discovered	1803	Smithson Tennant
palladium and rhodium discovered	1803	William Wollaston
iridium discovered	1804	Smithson Tennant
platinum isolated in a workable form	1805	William Wollaston
cadmium discovered	1817	Friedrich Stromeyer
ruthenium discovered	1828	Gottfried Osann
meitnerium, hassium, ununnilium, unununium, and ununbium first made	1982–1996	Institute for Heavy Ion Research, Germany

Further Reading and Useful Websites

Books

Fullick, Ann. *Science Topics: Chemicals in Action*. Chicago: Heinemann Library, 1999.

Oxlade, Chris. *Chemicals in Action* series, particularly *Metals; Atoms; Elements and Compounds*. Chicago: Heinemann Library, 2002.

Websites

WebElements™
http://www.webelements.com
An interactive periodic table crammed with information and photographs.

DiscoverySchool
http://school.discovery.com/students
Help for science projects and homework, and free science clip art.

Proton Don
http://www.funbrain.com/periodic
The fun periodic table quiz!

Creative Chemistry
http://www.creative-chemistry.org.uk
An interactive chemistry site with fun practical activities, quizzes, puzzles, and more.

Mineralogy Database
http://www.webmineral.com
Lots of useful information about minerals, including color photographs and information about their chemistry.

Index